To: _____

From: _____

Other books by Gregory E. Lang:

Why a Daughter Needs a Dad

Why a Daughter Needs a Mom

Why a Son Needs a Dad

Why a Son Needs a Mom

Why I Love Grandma

Why I Love Grandpa

Why I Chose You

Why I Love You

Why I Need You

Why We Are a Family

Why We Are Friends

Brothers and Sisters

Simple Acts

Love Signs

Life Maps

Thank You, Mom

Thank You, Dad

WHY I STILL LOVE YOU

100 reasons

GREGORY E. LANG

CUMBERLAND HOUSE

NASHVILLE, TENNESSEE

WHY I STILL LOVE YOU
Published by Cumberland House Publishing, Inc.
431 Harding Industrial Drive
Nashville, TN 37211

ISBN-13: 978-1-58182-598-5
ISBN-10: 1-58182-598-6

Cover design: Unlikely Suburban Design
Text design: Lisa Taylor
Interior Photos: Gregory E. Lang
Cover Photo: Stockbyte

Printed in Canada
1 2 3 4 5 6 7 8 — 13 12 11 10 09 08 07

To Jill

Though a few years have passed, I am just as excited about us as when I first laid eyes on you. I will love you always, and I am still yours, irreversibly.

INTRODUCTION

A little more than a year ago my wife, Jill, and I sat with members of my family in a crowded room and watched a man and a woman dance. He, agile and with deft feet, did most of the dancing. She, weakened by a long-term illness, smiled as he swirled around her. He held her hand to steady her and looked at her with love in his eyes, while watching her closely for signs of fatigue. They were my aunt and uncle, and it was their fiftieth wedding anniversary.

Uncle Mike and Aunt Mary Jean met in church at a youth fellowship event. They were each other's first date; they had been each other's only companion since that evening so long ago. Theirs was the longest romantic history of any couple I've ever known, except for my parents, who met over fifty-eight years ago.

As Jill and I watched my aunt and uncle dance, we were touched by the evidence of their enduring love, and yet we were somewhat saddened by a realization. We have been married only a few years; our union, a subsequent marriage for each of us, occurred when we were well into our midlife. We wish we had met sooner, fearing as we do that though we plan to spend the rest of our lives together, that time will be, indeed, too short. We will never see a fiftieth anniversary.

I tried to reassure my wife that evening by promising her I would make sure we packed as many wonderful experiences and romantic memories as we could into the time we would be given. I was confident in my promise because I have had good teachers to show me how to nurture a lasting marriage.

In addition to my aunt and uncle and my parents, I have many other relatives who have also enjoyed long-lasting marriages. It is from my older relatives that I have learned to never stop courting and flirting with your spouse, to reciprocate every gesture of affection and act of kindness shown to you, and always attempt to steal a kiss when it is least expected, no matter who may be watching. By watching my older married relatives interact, I have tried to discover the secrets of having a lasting marriage.

I think everyone has an older-generation couple in their family they look to as role models. We think of these people as role models because we see what we think are perfect or near-perfect marriages. We do not really know what their troubles might have been during their many years together, but we know that no matter what they were, the relationship endured the challenges they faced—the couple survived intact. Somehow they figured out how to overcome differences and stay focused on the love shared rather than the frustration or hurt that might have occurred. I wanted to know how to do that, too.

I think one of the secrets of a lasting marriage is to understand that no matter how much you love someone, your relationship will not be perfect. It will be tested, sometimes more than once. Love involves risk, hard work, and compromise, even sometimes tears, but with the understanding that while such difficulties will arise, they can be offset by the goodwill and good memories that have been intentionally created in advance.

An additional secret, and one that I hope will become conventional wisdom, is to also understand that to conquer the test is to reach a deeper, more enduring connection that helps the relationship survive, if not thrive. *More* love is the reward for remaining persistent and diligent in protecting and preserving the union.

Uncle Mike and Aunt Mary Jean's relationship thrived. I do not know what difficulties they faced, but I am certain that whatever they might have been, none were so great that they were remembered on the dance floor during that evening of celebration of their fifty-year marriage. Nor were they remembered one winter night a year later, when my aunt died at home.

That night her oldest son, another cousin, and I, the first three grandchildren of our clan, stood at the foot of their bed and watched as my uncle held the body of his wife of fifty-one years. He stroked her hair, sang love songs to her, proclaimed her to be his best friend, and said to us, "I'm so glad she can finally rest."

In the thirty minutes my cousins and I stood there bearing witness to this remarkable display of unselfish love, I learned what I now think is the real secret of lasting marriage. My uncle's thoughts were not of the pain of his great loss, but of the absence of her pain, that which had gripped her for so long. In his heart, in his life, she came first.

And so it is. The secret to having a lasting marriage is that in all matters of life, the spouse comes first. It is the best, indeed the only, evidence that demonstrates, "You are more important to me than I am." That is unselfish love. When both spouses abide by this moral, there is no fracture that could threaten the marriage, no obstacle that cannot be overcome, no limit to the love that can be enjoyed.

I left the house that early morning with a new perspective on committing oneself in marriage. When I next laid eyes on Jill, I saw her differently. I held her differently. I loved her differently—I loved her more. I pledged then not to waste an opportunity to tell and show her, "I love you more than myself."

I first set out to write this book to celebrate long-term, committed, romantic relationships, to create a gift for a couple who wanted to tell each other, "I'm still so in love with you that I would marry you again tomorrow!" For them, I hope these pages resonate and are shared together with a laugh and a smile.

I also wrote this book for couples who will weather storms, be it because of specific unforeseen events or just the inevitable changes that occur over the course of a lifetime. For them, I hope this book might be the perfect gift for one to communicate to the other that they want the relationship to endure. May these words and photos inspire them to embrace their romantic history and recommit to one another with hope and optimism.

Finally, I sat down to finish this book soon after having the privilege of witnessing the passing of my aunt. I conclude it now with a renewed promise to my wife: Jill, you come first in my life and in my heart. To give evidence of that promise, I will make sure that on the last day we spend together, you will know not only why I loved you in the beginning, but why I continued to love you till then.

WHY I STILL LOVE YOU

I still love you because

even after all this time, you still find me irresistible.

I still love you because

you have never stopped doing the sweet little things that delight me.

I still love you because

you have kept all the secrets I have confided in you.

I still love you because . . .

you calm me down when I am flipping out.

you try to anticipate my needs, and then fulfill them in abundance.

you have devoted yourself to helping make my dreams come true.

when I am facing a difficult challenge, you carry
as much of my burden as you can.

I still love you because

when I reach for you, you still move closer.

I still love you because

day in and day out, nothing is more important to us
than being together.

I still love you because . . .

even when we are apart, you let me know I am
in your heart and thoughts.

we share the belief that too much cannot be asked of each other.

you consider how things will affect me before you act.

you demand nothing from me, and gratefully accept
whatever I can give.

I still love you because

we made a home and a family together, a history of our own.

I still love you because

the way you look at me makes it obvious to others

that you are in love with me.

I still love you because . . .

you never talk about me in anything less than
the most flattering and affectionate ways.

you still write love letters to me. I've saved them all.

you don't mind rubbing my tired and aching bones.

you still carry my old glamour photo everywhere you go.

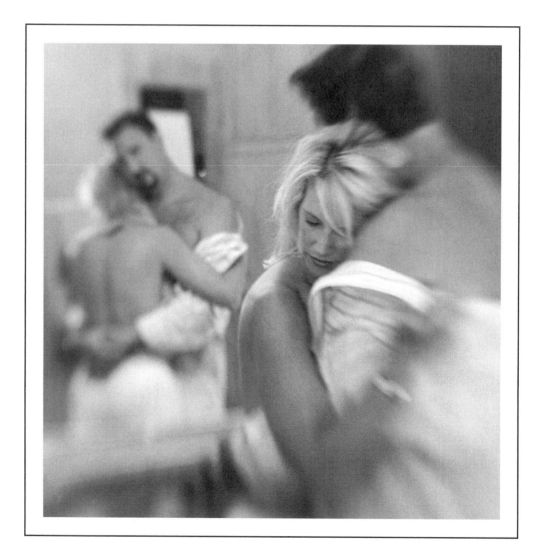

I still love you because

if we have a disagreement, you always insist we kiss
and make up as quickly as possible.

I still love you because

your lust for me hasn't faded a bit.

I still love you because

you slow dance with me whenever I ask.

I still love you because

you never grow tired of hearing me say, "I love you."

I still love you because

our times together have been the best times of my life.

I still love you because

you never tire of me leaning on you for comfort and support.

I still love you because . . .

when I need you, you are quick to drop everything to come to my aid.

you have never been indifferent to my fears and concerns.

you have never put yourself in situations that made
me uncomfortable or embarrassed.

you know how to say the difficult things
to me without hurting my feelings.

I still love you because

you have found new ways to keep intimacy in our relationship.

I still love you because

you always tell and show me that I make you happy.

I still love you because

you continue to give all of yourself to me.

I still love you because

you understand things about me that others
have never been able to figure out.

I still love you because . . .

you have never stopped courting me,
and never stopped flirting with me.

your compliments are always sincere, never a cliché.

you still attempt to sneak a kiss from me when it is least expected.

you always notice when I change something about my appearance.

I still love you because

we always pull together for the benefit of our family.

I still love you because

you always listen to me, even if you've heard it all before.

I still love you because

you have always loved and accepted me for who I am,
not who you hoped I might become.

I still love you because . . .

you don't mind reminding me of the things I have forgotten.

you always ask me questions before jumping to conclusions.

when you have important decisions to make, you ask me for advice.

you encourage me to talk about the events of my day
and what is on my mind.

I still love you because

we respect each other's differences but celebrate
the many things we have in common.

I still love you because

with you I have a profound sense of belonging and importance.

I still love you because . . .

you have helped me to better understand myself.

you accept my limitations without pointing them out to me.

you forgive me for the times that I unintentionally
hurt or offended you.

you work for compromise rather than fight to be right.

I still love you because

you reserve private time for us in every day.

I still love you because

you reciprocate every gesture of affection
and act of kindness I show to you.

I still love you because

you are thoughtful and diligent about keeping romance
and excitement in our relationship.

I still love you because . . .

you have never taken out your frustrations on me.

you reassure me whenever I need it, no matter how
often that might be.

you have always shown your trust in me, and even more importantly,
have always been trustworthy.

you seize every opportunity to tell others how much I mean to you.

I still love you because

you are always honest with me about your feelings,
and are equally concerned about mine.

I still love you because

you have shown a genuine interest in the things
that are important to me.

I still love you because

your words and actions continue to make me feel
desirable and attractive.

I still love you because

you have worked hard to stay in good health
and physical shape for both of us.

I still love you because

you are as thoughtful toward me now as you were
when first trying to win my heart.

I still love you because

we have proven ourselves to be stronger together
than we are apart.

I still love you because . . .

even as you've changed, you've made sure at your core
you remained the person I fell in love with.

you never fail to recognize and thank me for what I do for you.

we have always worked together to overcome our challenges.

you have put thought and effort into assuring my future well-being.

I still love you because

your desire for me has remained unfettered and unconditional.

I still love you because

you have never grown tired of my desire for your attention.

I still love you because

you have never expressed any regret about the time
we have spent together.

I still love you because . . .

you are always happy to see me at the end of the day.

you never let life or work get so busy that you forget about me.

you never hesitate to indulge me; you've spoiled me rotten.

you do so much for me but never make me feel indebted to you.

I still love you because

you are proud to be seen with me, no matter how
I've changed over the years.

I still love you because

we agreed upon and have accomplished important goals
in our life together.

I still love you because

you have saved everything I have ever given you.

I still love you because . . .

you are the first to step in and protect me.

I can look to you for guidance when I don't know what to do.

you know all my shortcomings and weaknesses
but never exploit them.

it never occurs to you that there might have been
someone better for you than me.

I still love you because

you continue to find a way to make me feel wanted
each and every day.

I still love you because . . .

you have willingly made so many sacrifices for my benefit.

you have helped me to become a better person than I might have been if left to my own devices.

you know when to laugh at me, and when to give comfort instead.

in times of sorrow or frustration, you have been there to wipe away my tears.

I still love you because

you always smile at me when our eyes meet.

I still love you because

you eagerly accept all the affection I want to give you.

I still love you because

you have always been faithful to the promises

we made to each other.

I still love you because . . .

you know what I meant to say, even if I didn't say it.
I think you can read my mind.

you have made me an equal partner in everything you do.

you understand where I am weak, and you
are my strength in those places.

you have the concern and the will to confront me when I am wrong.

I still love you because

you have never caused me heartache.

I still love you because . . .

you always forget after you have forgiven me.

I always receive more from you than I have asked for.

together we have the resolve to always improve ourselves so that we may give even more to one another.

like me, you believe a goodnight kiss should be the last event of every day.

I still love you because

on my blue days, you'll stop at nothing to cheer me up.

I still love you because

you gave me your heart, and never asked to have it back.

Acknowledgments

This book could not have been written without the trust and openness of many couples. I offer a heartfelt thanks to the men and women who shared their love stories with me, who overcame their modesty in order to let me capture intimate moments in photographs, and who helped me stay true to the vision of this book: that there really is one special person out there for each of us. I was deeply touched by the sincerity, commitment, and affection I witnessed in the time I spent with all of you.

I also wish to thank Ron Pitkin, my publisher, and the staff at Cumberland House, including my editor, Lisa Taylor, who once more helped me to make this book the best it could be, as well as all the other books we have completed together in the last five years. I hope you will agree with me that in getting these books out into the world, we have done something very special. I feel blessed to have been a part of this effort.

To Contact the Author

write in care of the publisher:
Cumberland House Publishing
431 Harding Industrial Drive
Nashville, TN 37211

or email:
greg.lang@mindspring.com
www.gregoryelang.com